A PILGRIM
IN THE HOLY LAND

Fr. Godfrey O.F.M.

Published by Palphot Ltd.

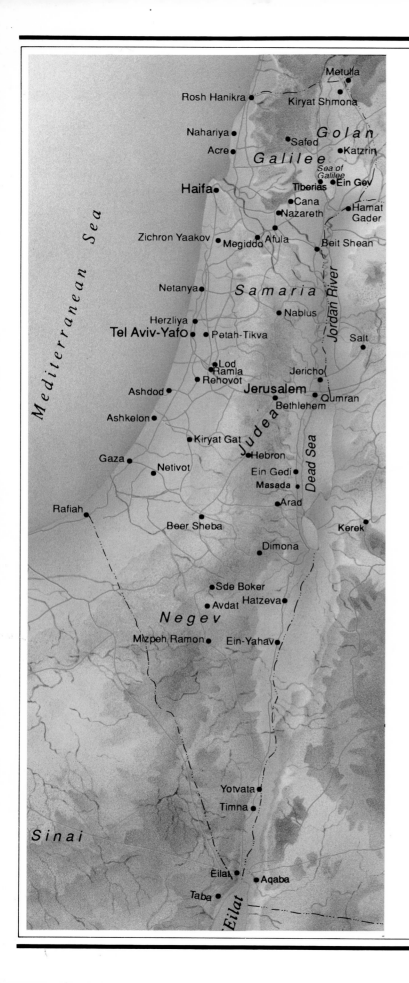

CONTENTS

Photographers: Garo Nalbandian and others
Aerial photographs: Duby Tal and Moni Haramati

ISBN 965-280-063-5

INTRODUCTION

By Rev. Fr. Godfrey Kloetzli O.F.M., K.C.H.S., S.Ch.L.J., M.A.

As a resident in the Middle East for some thirty years, since 1945, I have grown to love the Holy Land as my real home. Our beloved Catholic Patriarch of Jerusalem, Archbishop James Beltritti, so often stresses that every Christian has two native lands, the one of his birth and the Holy Land, especially Jerusalem. As Christians, Jerusalem is the birthplace of our faith and the Mother of all Churches. Thus, a book dedicated to bringing the Holy Land to the eyes of all is something very much to be desired. True there are already many such publications, but there can never be sufficient.

The best way to know the Holy Land is through a personal visit. Only then does one truly grasp the reality of this blessed country and only then does one more fully understand the Gospels. It is indeed a great privilege to be present at some sacred spot and either read the Gospel connected with that site or listen to it being read by someone else. It bestows a gift on the reader or listener which can never be taken away.

The second way to know the Holy Land is by reading descriptions and seeing pictures. As it is truly said, "One picture is worth a thousand words," so a picture book of the Holy Land is often worth many volumes of lengthy prose. John Chavoushian has gathered together in this book a magnificent selection of such pictures, many of them are quite beautifully composed. It is a great pleasure for me to leaf through the pages and I can most heartily recommend this book as a wonderful way of visiting the Land of Christ. Jesus chose this land into which to be born and live His life, His Mother, His first followers and the infant Church were all of this Land. We should cherish it also and savour each and every scene as it is unfolded before us. If you have had the privilege of actually visiting this land, it will serve to help you to relive those wonderful days.

I thank John for a beautiful piece of work and ask God to bless him for it.

May this book bring much joy and understanding to many people.

Fr. Godfrey, O.F.M.

**The Basilica of the Annunciation –
Nazareth** *(see p. 4)*
*"And in the sixth month the Angel Gabriel was
sent from God into a city of Galilee, named
Nazareth."* (Luke I:26).
*"And, behold, thou shalt conceive in thy
womb, and bring forth a son, and shalt call his
name Jesus."* (Luke I:31).

The central altar and two side altars (*see p. 5*)

Painting of the Annunciation (*facing page*)

Mary's Well (*right*)

The spring which issues from the interior of the Church of St. Gabriel flows into the heart of Nazareth. According to the Greek Orthodox tradition the Angel Gabriel met the Virgin Mary by this spring. The Virgin Mary took water for her household needs from this well.

The crypt of the Basilica of the Annunciation (*below*)

This is all that remains of the former churches built on the spot. On the marble altar is the following inscription: **Verbum caro hic factum est** (The Word was here made flesh). Near the altar stands an ancient column which traditionally marks the spot where the Angel Gabriel appeared to the Virgin Mary.

Nazareth *(and facing page)*

A general view of Nazareth which is dominated by the Basilica of the Annunciation. The city is located in a valley in Southern Galilee. Joseph and his wife Mary lived in Nazareth and Jesus spent His childhood there.

"And He came and dwelt in a city called Nazareth: that it might be fulfilled which was spoken by the prophets, he shall be called a Nazarene."
(Matthew 2:23)

In the first centuries A.D. Nazareth was populated only by Jews, but with the strengthening of the Roman Empire, the number of Christians living there grew. From the fourth century onwards, churches were built on the sites which were connected with Jesus and the Virgin Mary.

Today the population of Nazareth is mixed between Christians, Moslems and Jews. The Christians belong to various denominations: Orthodox, Roman Catholic, Greek Catholic, Maronite, Anglican, Copt, Armenian, Baptist and other Protestant sects. There are many churches, monasteries, convents, hostels, hospitals and schools maintained by the various denominations.

The present Basilica which was designed by the Italian architect, Prof. Giovanni Muzio, was completed in 1969. It is the fifth church built on the spot where the Angel Gabriel stood when he prophesied to the Virgin Mary that she would conceive a child. Remains of the first church were discovered during excavations which were started on the site in 1955. The second church was built during the Byzantine period; the third at the beginning of the 12th century and the fourth was completed in 1877.

The Church of The Visitation – Ein Karem

"And Mary arose in those days, and went into the hill country with haste into a city of Judah, and entered into the house of Zacharias, and saluted Elisabeth." (Luke I:39-40)

Ein Karem is a village situated 7 kilometres south-west of Jerusalem. According to tradition, Ein Karem is the "city of Judah" which is associated with the life of John the Baptist. Here Zacharias, John the Baptist's father, had his summer home, and here the Virgin Mary visited her cousin Elisabeth. The Church of the Visitation was built on the spot where the house was situated. The present Church of the Visitation was built in 1935 by the architect Barluzzi on the remains of former churches, the first of which was built in the fourth century A.D. and later destroyed. Inside the church there is a fresco depicting the visit of the Virgin Mary and below are the altar and the ancient well. *(facing page)* In the crypt of the church there is a rock where traditionally the infant John was hidden from the soldiers of the tyrant Herod.

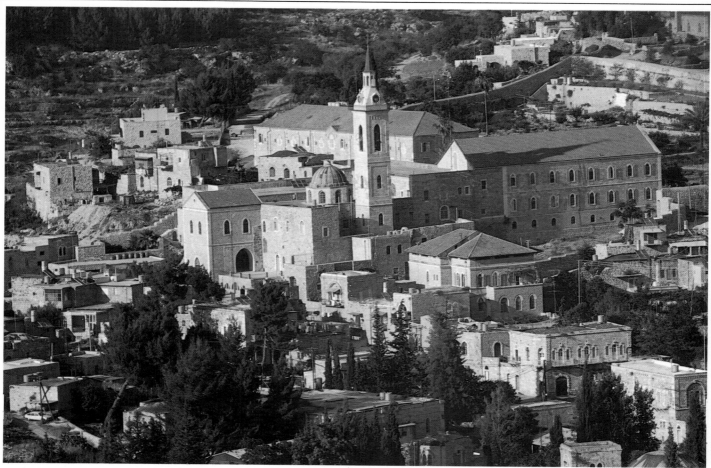

The Church of John the Baptist is in the centre of Ein Karem (above). The first Church was built in the fifth century A.D. A beautiful mosaic floor from that period has survived, it depicts peacocks, birds and flowers.

Below
The Grotto of the Benedictus, under whose altar is a star marking the place where John the Baptist was born.

Bethlehem – General View *(facing – p. 13)*
Bethlehem was originally called Ephratah (Ephrath) (Gen. 35:16 and Ruth 4:11). It is revered as the birthplace of David (1 Samuel 17:12) and Jesus (Matthew 2:5). Today Bethlehem is a busy town inhabited by many Christian Arabs who are skilled craftsmen and artisans.

The Shepherd's Field Church *(facing – p. 13)*
East of Bethlehem, in the village of Beit Sahur is the Shepherd's Field. This is the spot where the Angel appeared to the shepherds and announced the birth of Jesus (Luke 2:8).

Interior of the Shepherd's Field Church *(overleaf – p. 14)*
Above – left
Fresco depicting the angel announcing the birth of Jesus to the shepherds.
Above – right
A fresco which depicts the birth of Jesus.
Below
The Grotto of the Shepherds.

(Previous page 15)
Shepherds tending their flocks in the fields near Bethlehem as in biblical times.

Above
Overshadowed by the massive stone walls of the Basilica of the Nativity is the Door of Humility – the small doorway to the church. This entrance was lowered by partly sealing the Crusader arch sometime during the seventeenth century to ensure that Muslims could not enter the church riding their horses. The visitor of today must bend almost double to gain admission to the church.

Below
A well preserved remnant of the original mosaic floor showing the intricate geometric design and subtle colours used.

The Basilica of The Nativity, Bethlehem

"Now when Jesus was born in Bethlehem of Judaea in the days of Herod the King, behold there came Wise Men from the East to Jerusalem." (Matthew 2:1)
Bethlehem, as is related in the Gospel of Matthew 2:1 and in the Gospel of Luke 2:1-15, is the birthplace of Jesus.
The Gospel of Luke tells us that before the birth of Jesus, the Roman authorities ordered a population census in the land and therefore Jesus' parents moved from Nazareth to Bethlehem because Joseph was of the lineage of David and Bethlehem is the "City of David". Joseph and Mary could not find room in an inn so Jesus was born in a cave that was used as a stable. Above the cave was built a magnificent church – the Basilica of the Nativity.

(contd. on page 20)

The first church was built in the first half of the fourth century A.D. on the initiative of the Byzantine Emperor Constantine and his mother, the Empress Helena. This church was partially
destroyed in the Samaritan Revolt of the sixth century. The present church renovated built in the year 530 A.D. by Justinian. From the exterior it looks like a fortress. The entrance is low and narrow in order to protect it from the Moslem invaders and to prevent them from entering on horseback. The wooden door was built by the Armenian King Hetron in 1272 A.D.
Most churches were destroyed during the Persian invasion of the 7th century A.D., but apparently the Church of the Nativity was saved from desecration because of the mosaic then on the facade of the church. The Three Wise Men who came to pay homage to the baby Jesus (Matthew 2:2) were depicted wearing Persian clothing; it is believed that this stopped the Persians from destroying the church.

Bethlehem

Above (Previous pages 18 and 19)
The interior of the Justinian Basilica in the Church of the Nativity.

Below (p. 18)
One of the two stairways to the Grotto of the Nativity in the Church of the Nativity.

Below (p. 19)
The silver star in the Grotto of the Nativity. This denotes the spot where Jesus is thought to have been born. The inscription reads: **Hic De Virgine Maria Jesus Christus Natus Est** – Here Jesus Christ was born of the Virgin Mary.

The Church of St. Catherine-Christmas Eve

(facing page)
The interior of the Latin Church of St. Catherine. The church was built in 1881 next to the Church of the Nativity. In this church on Christmas Eve, the Latin Patriarch officiates at Midnight Mass.
Pilgrims come from all over the world to take part in this ancient Christmas service.

Facing page – above
Church steeples and a belltower in Bethlehem.

Facing page – below
Arabs riding their camels in the vicinity of Bethlehem, reminiscent of the "Three Wise Men."

Bethlehem, the milk grotto
Above
The exterior of the Milk Grotto.

Below
The interior of the Milk Grotto which commemorates the Christian doctrine of the Divine Maternity of the Virgin Mary.

The Hill of Herodian – Aerial View *(overleaf p. 24)*
The fortress of Herod is located 7 kilometres south-east of Bethlehem. Herodian, one of many fortresses built by Herod, was built as a refuge from his many enemies in Jerusalem. In archaeological excavations that were carried out at Herodian, remains of palaces, fortification towers, bath-houses and an aqueduct bringing water from afar were found. Before his death, Herod asked to be buried at Herodian. According to Josephus, he was indeed buried there.

When Herod heard of the birth of the baby Jesus, he feared for his sovereignity. Angrily he commanded the killing of all the male children in Bethlehem up to the age of two years. A painting in a church in Ein Karem portrays the slaughter of an infant.

The Flight into Egypt *(facing page)*

Joseph, the Virgin Mary and the Infant Jesus on their way to Egypt, fleeing from Herod. A model of "The Flight into Egypt" in the Milk Grotto near the Basilica of the Nativity.

"And when they were departed, Behold, The Angel of the Lord appeared to Joseph in a dream, saying, 'Arise, and take the young Child and His Mother, and flee into Egypt, and bide thou there until I bring thee word: for Herod will seek the young Child to destroy Him.' When he arose, he took the young Child and His Mother by night, and departed into Egypt." (Matthew 2:13-14)

The Tomb of Rachel

"And Rachel died, and was buried on the way to Ephrath, which is Bethlehem. And Jacob set a pillar upon her grave: That is the pillar of Rachel's grave unto this day." (Genesis 35:19-20)

The Tomb of Rachel, a small domed structure is venerated by Jews, Christians and Moslems. To this day Jews come to pray and ask mercy in times of trouble.

Solomon's Pools (*facing p. 26*)
Three huge triple reservoirs
known as "Solomon's Pools"
after his statement: *"I made
me pools of water to irrigate a
grove of growing trees."*
(Ecclesiastes 2:6) The pools
were constructed at the time of
Herod. The rain water which
collected from the surrounding
hills was directed through
aqueducts, thus supplying
Jerusalem with water
throughout the year. To this
day the system is still in use.

Above
**St. Mary of the Hortus
Conclusus** – from which the
arabic name Wadi Artas is
derived. Close to Solomon's
Pools is a monastery which was
built in the nineteenth century
by an Argentinian Bishop.

Below
Sheep grazing near Bethlehem

Overleaf (p. 28 and p. 29)
**Market scenes of Bethlehem
today**

Above

The Holy Family
This painting in the Church of St. Joseph
in Nazareth portrays the every day life of
the Holy Family. After their flight to
Egypt they returned to their home town of
Nazareth in the Galilee. (Luke 2:39-40)

Below
The Grotto of the Holy Family
Underground area of Joseph's home,
possibly his workshop. The mouth of a silo
can be seen on the left. The pilaster on the
right is modern.

Top left
Entrance to Greek Orthodox Church of St. Gabriel.

Top right
Interior of St. Joseph's Church – Nazareth.

Lower left
Mary's Well, next to the Church of St. Gabriel – Nazareth.

Lower right
The market in Nazareth.

Facing (page 33)
"The Good Shepherd"

Cana

It was in Cana that Jesus performed His first miracle of converting water into wine at a wedding. Jesus, His Mother and His Disciples were guests at the wedding. (John 2:1-11)

Right
A painting showing Jesus at the wedding in Cana.

Below
The Church of The Miracle at Cana

The present church is constructed on the ruins of a church built in the 6th century A.D. Inside there is a mosaic floor from the 4th century. Many young Christian couples come here to celebrate their weddings.

Facing page – above
"The House of the Wedding" in the crypt of the Church at Cana. A Roman water jug symbolizes the larger ones used to hold water at the time of the first miracle.

Nain

A little over 3 kilometres south of Mt. Tabor is the peaceful village of Nain ("Beauty"). Here Jesus performed the miracle of the raising of a widow's son. (Luke 7:11-15).

Mount Tabor

This is not mentioned by name in the New Testament, but according to tradition, this is the high "mountain set apart" which Christ ascended with the apostles Peter, James and John. He was transfigured before them, his face shining like the sun, and his clothing a brilliant white.

(Facing page 37)
The front of the Basilica of the Transfiguration which was built on the ruins of the Byzantine and Crusader churches in 1924 by the architect Antonio Barluzzi in the Roman-Syrian style of the 4th-7th centuries. A bust of Pope Paul VI commemorates his visit here in January 1964.

(Overleaf page 38)
Mt. Tabor – The Basilica of the Transfiguration

Above the main altar of the central apse in the Basilica of the Transfiguration a beautiful golden mosaic represents the Transfiguration. Christ in the centre is surrounded by the prophets Moses (on the left) and Elijah (on the right). Peter, James and John are depicted below.

(Overleaf page 39)
Aerial picture of the present church built on the ruins of the Byzantine and the Crusader churches.

Below
The entrance to the site

The fortified entrance gateway to the sanctuary of the Basilica of the Transfiguration overlooks the Jezreel Valley.

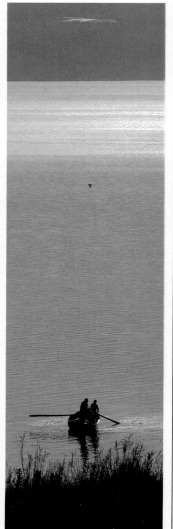

(Previous page 40)

Views of the Sea of Galilee

The calm and tranquility of the sparkling blue waters of the Sea of Galilee sometimes change to violent storms. The waters turn an angry grey as strong winds whip up small waves. Fishing is still an important occupation – as in biblical times.

Capernaum *(above)*

The ruins of the white limestone synagogue built in the typical Basilica style probably stand on the site of the original synagogue in which Jesus preached during his ministry in Galilee. The carved lintels are richly decorated with Jewish symbols.

Capernaum *(below)*

Birds eye view showing the remains of the synagogue, family living quarters and the new church covering Peter's house. The Sea of Galilee is in the background.

Above

External view of new church at Capernaum

A circular church has been erected over the traditional site of the house of Simon Peter, and the remains of the Byzantine church.

Below

Interior of the new church at Capernaum

The modern church is usually kept closed. It is only opened by special request for groups of Catholic pilgrims who wish to celebrate Mass.

(Facing page 43)

Remains of the ancient synagogue on which are carved Jewish symbols – such as the Menorah and the carriage for carrying the Holy Ark of the Covenant.

Facing page – below
Millstones.

A mosaic of the Loaves and the Fishes – symbol of the miracle which Jesus performed in order to feed the multitude who had come to hear Him preach. *"But Jesus said unto them. They need not depart: give ye them to eat. And they said unto Him, We have here but five loaves, and two fishes. He said, Bring them hither to me. And He commanded the multitude to sit down on the grass, and took the five loaves, and the two fishes, and looking up to heaven, He blessed, and brake, and gave the loaves to His Disciples, and the Disciples to the multitude. And they did all eat, and were filled: and they took up the fragments that remained twelve baskets full. And they that had eaten were about five thousand men, besides women and children."* (Matthew 14:16-21)

Below
Modern version of the mosaic.

Tabgha – The exterior of the Church of the Loaves and the Fishes
Built in the 4th century this simple church commemorates one of the most well known miracles that Jesus performed – the "feeding of the multitude".

Tabgha – The interior of the Church of the Loaves and the Fishes
The edifice was designed to reflect the style of a Byzantine church, using many of the original mosaics.

Above
Dalmanutha

Dalmanutha (Mark 8:10)
*he...... came into the parts of
Dalmanutha.* Traditionally
this is where Jesus sighed for
mankind. The place of
meditation, on the west side of
the Sea of Galilee, near
Magdala, is marked with a
great cross facing the peaceful
waters.

(Facing – page 46)

Well preserved mosaic – Symbol of Redemption

This beautiful mosaic in the Benedictine Church dates from
the 4th century. The small bird represents man, the snake
represents Satan, and the flamingo represents Christ. The
three figures together depict the Symbol of Redemption.

Above

Aerial view of Tabgha and the Church of St. Peter's Primacy

The church is built on a rock. It commemorates the election
of Peter as head of the future church. Peter's former name
was Simon – Jesus changed his name to Peter (Petra – a rock,
in Latin). Here he said to Peter, *"Feed my lambs, feed my
sheep"*. (John 21:15-19).

Below

Statue overlooking the Sea of Galilee

This statue depicts Christ, after the Resurrection, appearing
for the third time before his disciples. According to the
Gospel story, as told in John (21:1–17) Jesus reinstated Peter.

Above

Pilgrims outside the Church of St. Peter's Primacy, Tabgha

The simple church was built next to ancient steps leading down to the waterline.

Below

Interior of the Church of St. Peter's Primacy, Tabgha

The stark simplicity of the Church of St. Peter's Primacy is enhanced by the black basalt rocks used in its construction. Built by the Franciscans in 1938, on Byzantine foundations it encloses the rock known as Mensa Christi – the Table of Christ. Here Jesus *"showed himself again to his disciples at the sea of Tiberias"*, (John 21:1), and they ate together.

1

2

3

4

Above (Previous page 49)
View to the Sea of Galilee from the cloisters of the Church of the Beatitudes.

Below (Previous page 49)
The Church of the Beatitudes
Situated atop the Mount of Beatitudes overlooking the Sea of Galilee the octagonal shaped chapel of the Church of the Beatitudes marks the spot where Jesus delivered the Sermon on the Mount. (Matthew 5:3–10). Antonio Barluzzi built the church in 1937. Collonaded cloisters surround the entire structure – offering a beautiful panoramic view of the Sea of Galilee.

Left:
1. *Blessed are the poor in spirit, for theirs is the Kingdom of Heaven.*
2. *Blessed are those who mourn, for they shall be comforted.*
3. *Blessed are the meek, for they shall inherit the earth.*
4. *Blessed are those who hunger and thirst for righteousness, for they shall be satisfied.*

5

6

7

Right

5. *Blessed are the merciful, for they shall obtain mercy.*
6. *Blessed are the pure in heart, for they shall see God.*
7. *Blessed are the peacemakers, for they shall be called the sons of God.*
8. *Blessed are those who are persecuted for righteousness sake, for theirs is the Kingdom of Heaven.*

Matthew 5:3–10.

(Facing page 50)
The High Altar in the Church of the Beatitudes

Above
Interior of the Church of the Beatitudes – The Cupola

On each window of the cupola is written part of the text of the eight Beatitudes, as spoken by Jesus when he delivered his Sermon on the Mount.

8

Left
Fishermen on the Sea of Galilee at sunset.

Top right
Ruins of the Church at Kursi
This is the site of the New Testament Gergesa or Gadara. A Byzantine monastery with a beautiful mosaic floor has been discovered.

Centre – right
A capital from the black basalt second century A.D. synagogue at Korazim.

The Galilee Boat

This ancient boat built with wooden joints was discovered during the drought year of 1985. It is believed to be a fisherman's boat dating from the later part of the first century B.C. to 70 A.D.

Caesarea Philippi (Banias)

Jesus visited Caesarea Philippi with His disciples. Here Jesus asked His disciples who the people thought He was and who they (the disciples) thought He was. And Simon Peter said that He was the Messiah. *"And Simon Peter answered and said, Thou art the Christ, the Son of the living God. Jesus answered: Blessed art thou, Simon, son of John… for thou art Peter and upon this rock (Petrus) I will build my church."* (Matthew 16)

Inset

The Grotto of the god Pan at the spring of Banias. From here springs one of the sources of the River Jordan. In the walls of the grotto are carved niches from the Roman period: in these niches were statues dedicated to the god of the wood.

Yardenit – The Place of Baptism

Amongst the pilgrim sites by the Sea of Galilee is Yardenit, the Place of Baptism, where the River Jordan leaves the lake, close to kibbutz Degania Aleph.

Countless pilgrims from far and wide gather here to immerse themselves in the holy waters of the River Jordan. Clad in white robes, all believe with devout sincerity that they are indeed following in the tradition of the scriptures; Jesus *"was baptized of John in Jordan"*. (Mark 1:9).

The River Jordan

Pilgrims taking part in a ceremony at the spot where Jesus was baptized.

Inset: A painting of the baptism of Jesus is to be found in the St. John the Baptist Church in Ein Karem.

Top left
The Spring of Elisha
Tradition connects this spring with the
Prophet Elisha. There is a
Greek Orthodox Church, St. Elisha's Church,
in Jericho.

Below right

The Sycamore Tree – Jericho
Travelling back to Jerusalem, Jesus passed
through Jericho. Amongst the crowd of
people waiting to catch a glimpse of Him was a
small man named Zaccheus. In order to get a
better view he climbed into the sycamore tree.
The story of how Zaccheus received salvation
is told in Luke. (Luke 19:5-9)

Jericho – City of Dates
(facing page 57)
Tel-es-Sultan: the walls of ancient Jericho at
Tel-es-Sultan, which were discovered during
archaeological digs started in 1868 and
continued spasmodically until 1954. The walls
date back 10,000 years.

(Facing page 58)
The Mount of Temptation – Quarantel Monastery *"And immediately the Spirit driveth Him into the wilderness. And He was there in the wilderness forty days, tempted of Satan; and was with the wild beasts; and the angels ministered unto Him."* (Mark 1:12) On the side of a mountain west of Jericho is the Greek Orthodox Monastery called the Monastery of Quarantel or the Monastery of the Temptation. According to tradition, it was here that Jesus isolated Himself and fasted forty days. At the top of the mountain are the remains of a chapel which marks the spot where Satan tempted Jesus. (Matthew 4:1-11 and Luke 4:1-3)

Above
The Hulda Steps in the southern wall of the Temple Mount. These led into the courtyard at the time when the Second Temple was standing and were in fact the very steps used by Jesus.

Below
The Pinnacle of the Temple in Jerusalem to which Satan brought Jesus in order to tempt Him for the third time. (Luke 4:9-13)

Overleaf (p.60)
Scroll fragment – Qumran *(top)*
Part of the hidden treasure of manuscripts and scrolls found at Qumran on the western shore of the Dead Sea.

Qumran (below)

The ruins of a once flourishing settlement and writings of over 2,000 years ago were discovered at Qumran – situated at the lowest point of the earth's surface in the Great Rift Valley. Between 150 B.C. and 68 A.D., the community of the Essenes found in Qumran an ideally secluded place for prayer and contemplation. Exiled from the temptations of the city, high up on a limestone plateau overlooking the Dead Sea they awaited the coming of the Lord – according to their interpretation of the words of the prophet Isaiah. (Isaiah 40:3)

Ruins and Caves at Qumran

The most stunning biblical archaeological find of this century took place in 1947 when a young Bedouin boy unknowingly discovered a hoard of ancient manuscripts in a cave at Qumran.

Excavations led by Roland de Vaux have uncovered remains from five periods when the settlement of Qumran was inhabited. The vast scriptorium bears evidence of the scribes work – transcribing texts from the Bible and other works written during the Second Temple era, on to leather, papyrus and copper.

When Titus and the Roman legions arrived at Jericho, the Essenes fled, hiding their scrolls in the nearby caves. The desert kept their secret for almost 2,000 years. The discovery of the scrolls had an enormous effect on the Christian world as they were transcribed during the time of the birth of Christianity. The scrolls which were discovered at Qumran are now housed in the Shrine of the Book at the Israel Museum in Jerusalem. (See page 134)

Ein Gedi

"And David went up from thence, and dwelt in the strongholds at Ein Gedi." (Samuel 1:23-29)

Ein Gedi *(right)* is an ancient settlement near the shores of the Dead Sea. It is famous for its springs and waterfalls. It was one of the desert settlements of the Tribe of Judah and it was to Ein Gedi that David fled from King Saul.

Below
An Ibex

A member of the mountain goat family. These ibexes are to be found in the Judean Desert, especially around the caves and cliffs of Ein Gedi.

Ein Gedi means *"The Spring of the Young Goat."*

Crystallized mounds of salt on the shores of the Dead Sea

Massada *Overleaf (p.64)*

Massada, situated above the Dead Sea, was one of the fortresses which were built and fortified by Herod the Great. Here the few surviving Jewish patriots who took part in the Jewish Revolt against the Romans gathered to make their last stand.

The Zealots, led by Eleazar ben Yair were besieged for three

years by the Romans. Realizing that it was impossible to hold out any longer, the 967 defenders committed suicide, preferring to die as free men rather than be taken into captivity by the Romans. Excavations led by the late Professor Yigael Yadin uncovered the remains of the fortress, with its storerooms, cisterns, bath-houses, palaces, synagogue and ritual baths.

facing page (p. 65)

Remains of the palace and the buildings excavated at Massada

Top left: Part of the Byzantine Church.

Centre left: Herodian mosaic.

Bottom left: Some of the storehouses.

Right: The lower terrace of Herod's Northern Hanging Palace.

Jerusalem – "Possession of Peace"

"If I forget thee, Oh, Jerusalem, let my right hand forget her cunning." (Psalms 137:5)

"Thus saith the Lord God; this is Jerusalem: I have set it in the midst of the nations." (Ezekiel 5:5)

The references and quotations about Jerusalem are innumerable. It is known as Jerusalem the Golden, the Sacred City, the City of Peace..... There is not another city that has been the cause of so many armed conflicts as Jerusalem. Holy sites, revered by the three great monotheistic faiths are a constant draw to pilgrims from all over the world.

Above

The fig tree that was cursed by Jesus during His last days on earth.

"And when He saw a fig tree in the way, He came to it and found nothing thereon, but leaves only, and said unto it. Let no fruit grow on thee henceforward forever and presently the fig withered away." (Matthew 11:19)

Below

The Temple Mount

A view of the Temple Mount and the Holy City of Jerusalem. In the centre of the Temple Mount is the Dome of the Rock (The Mosque of Omar).

The Tomb of Lazarus *(above)*

In the village of Bethany is a cave which, according to tradition, is the Tomb of Lazarus. Above the cave is a minaret of a Moslem mosque.

The Church of Lazarus – Bethany *(below)*

On the eastern slope of the Mount of Olives is the Arab village of El Azaryia. This is the ancient Bethany which Jesus passed on His way from Jericho to Jerusalem. Here Jesus performed the miracle of raising Lazarus from the dead. Lazarus was the brother of Martha and Mary Magdalene. (John 11:1-44)

The church was built by the architect Barluzzi on the ruins of previous churches. In the interior of the church are many mosaics, copies of frescoes painted by G. Vagarini. *(See pages 72-73)*

In the village there are other monasteries and churches.

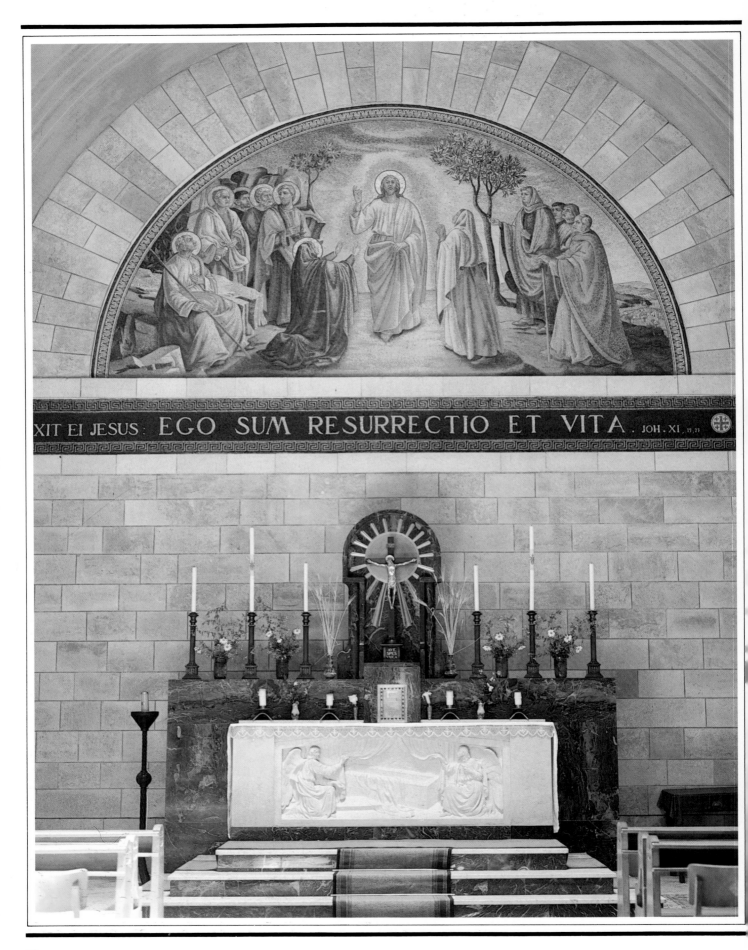

XIT EI JESUS: EGO SUM RESURRECTIO ET VITA . JOH . XI . 17, 23

DIXIT ILLI DOMINUS: MARTHA MARTHA SOLLICITA ES ET TURBARIS ERGA PLURIMA. Lc X,41

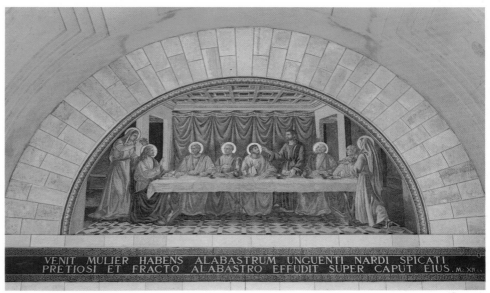

VENIT MULIER HABENS ALABASTRUM UNGUENTI NARDI SPICATI PRETIOSI ET FRACTO ALABASTRO EFFUDIT SUPER CAPUT EIUS. Mc XIV,3

PATER UT CREDANT QUIA TU ME MISISTI HAEC CUM DIXISSET VOCE MAGNA CLAMAVIT: LAZARE VENI FORAS. JOH XI,42

The Interior of the Church of Lazarus *(facing page)*

The main altar, above which is a mosaic depicting Martha and Mary speaking to Jesus.

Details of the mosaics

Jesus speaking to Lazarus' sisters, Martha and Mary. *(top)*

Jesus eating in Bethany at the house of Simon the Leper. *(centre)*

Jesus raising Lazarus from the dead. *(bottom)*

The Mount of Olives

The Church of the Pater Noster
Here Jesus taught His Disciples the Lord's Prayer – the
Pater Noster. On the walls of the church, the prayer is
written in over fifty languages.

Nuns and their pupils taking part in the Palm Sunday procession which starts at Bethphage on the slopes of the Mount of Olives.

Bethphage *(p. 72)*

A fresco above the main altar of the church at Bethphage which shows the entry of Jesus into Jerusalem riding on a young ass. *"And Jesus, when He had found a young ass, rode thereon: as it is written, etc."* (John 12:14) In the church is a stone said to bear the imprint of
Jesus' foot as He mounted the ass.

Bethphage – "House of Unripe Figs" *(Luke 19:1-4) (facing page 72)*

A settlement near Bethany on the road from Jerusalem to Jericho. This is believed to be the beginning of the descent from the Mount of Olives. (Matthew 21:1-3 and Mark 11:1-2)

Above
The Palm Sunday procession starting from Bethphage going to
Jerusalem.

Below left
The procession entering St. Stephen's Gate.

Below right
When the procession reaches Jerusalem the assembled pilgrims join in prayer.

Inside the Chapel of the Ascension (right) is the rock from which Jesus ascended to heaven. Pilgrims believe that one can see His footprint on the rock.

The Chapel of the Ascension *(below)*

An eight-sided building on the top of the Mount of Olives marking the traditional spot where Jesus ascended to heaven. In the background – the spire of the Russian Orthodox Church.

The City of David *(facing page – top)*

The southern wall of the Temple Mount and the Mosque of El-Aksa. Excavations outside the wall have uncovered the Hulda Steps from the Second Temple period. The Kidron Valley and the village of Silwan can be seen in the background.

Below

A view of Jerusalem with the eastern wall of the Temple Mount and the Golden Gate in the centre.

The Church of the Dormition

The Church of the Dormition on Mout Zion is the place where the Virgin Mary fell into eternal sleep. The church was built at the beginning of this century on the remains of previous churches built during the Byzantine and Crusader periods.

The Coenaculum *(facing page)*

The Room of the Last Supper on Mount Zion. This is where Jesus ate the Passover meal, the Last Supper. (Luke 22:7-38 and Mark 14:15-25)

In the Coenaculum is the place where Jesus washed the Disciples' feet.

Below

A wood and ivory effigy of the Virgin Mary on her deathbed in the crypt of the Church of the Dormition.

The Traditional Tomb of King David on Mount Zion

In the lower Chapel of the Church of the Coenaculum is the Tomb of King David. On the tomb are silver crowns from Torah scrolls brought to Israel from synagogues in the Diaspora which were destroyed with their communities during the Holocaust. Jews come to pray at the Tomb of David throughout the year, but especially at Shavuot (The Feast of Weeks), the date of David's death.

The Tomb of Absalom in the Kidron Valley

Tradition says this is the grave of Absalom (II Samuel 18), however it is generally accepted that this structure was erected some 700 years later during the period of the Second Temple.

The Kidron Valley – Valley of Jehoshaphat *(overleaf p.80)*

The Tomb of Absalom, the Church of All Nations and the Russian Orthodox Church of Mary Magdalene are starkly illuminated against the blackness of the night.

The Tomb of Zachariah and the Tomb of Bnei Hezir
(overleaf p.81)

When the Universal Resurrection is completed it is traditionally believed that trumpets will sound and the Last Judgement will take place in the Kidron Valley. For this reason the site has been a favoured burial place for Jews for thousands of years.

Dominus Flevit – "The Lord Wept" *(facing page)*

The Church of Dominus Flevit on the slopes of the Mount of Olives facing the Temple Mount. The present church was built on the ruins of an ancient church and marks the spot where Jesus wept over the city of Jerusalem which would be destroyed shortly. (Luke 19:41-44)

The window above the altar through which can be seen the Temple Mount and Jerusalem.

Right
One of the ancient olive trees in the Garden of Gethsemene.

The Church of All Nations – Gethsemene *(below)*
This church is also called the Basilica of the Agony. Jesus and His Disciples spent the last hours before His arrest in the Garden of Gethsemene. The present church was built in the early 1920's with contributions from twelve nations. It was built on the ruins of Byzantine and Crusader churches.

Interior of the Church of All Nations
(facing page)
Inside the church in front of the main altar is the traditional Rock of Agony upon which Jesus prayed the night before His arrest. The rock is surrounded by a crown of thorns of wrought iron. Above the altar is a painting depicting an angel comforting Jesus.

(Return to page 86, 87)

Top left
The Church of the Tomb of the Virgin Mary – *built by the Crusaders.*

Top right
Interior of the Church of the Tomb of the Virgin Mary.
In the church are altars dedicated to Joachim and Anne, the Virgin Mary's parents. Queen Melisanda who reigned during the Crusader period was also buried here.

Bottom picture
The interior of the crypt which marks the traditional place of the Virgin Mary's tomb.

(Facing page 88)
The Russian Church of St. Mary Magdalene
This church was built in 1888 by Czar Alexander III. The golden domes are typical of the Muscovite church style.

Above
The Pool of Siloam in the City of David was built by King Hezekiah; it was quarried out of the rock. It was to this pool that Jesus sent the blind man to wash. *"And said unto him. Go, wash in the Pool of Siloam. He went his way therefore, and washed, and came seeing."* (John 9:7)

Below
The water tunnel was cut out of the rock by King Hezekiah's workers in order to bring the waters of the Gihon spring inside the city walls in time of siege.

Right
The steps from Hasmonean times in the courtyard of the Church of St. Peter in Gallicantu. The steps connected the City of David with the Upper City (Mt. Zion) in the Second Temple period.

The Church of St. Peter in Gallicantu *(below and facing page)*
A modern church that was built in 1931 on the accepted site of the House of Caiaphas, the High Priest at the time of the arrest of Jesus. It is traditionally believed that this is the place where Peter denied his Master, according to the prophecy of Jesus – *"Before the cock crow, thou shalt deny me thrice."* (Mark 14:66-72 and Luke 22:61)

The Pools of Bethesda (facing page)

In 1871 excavations carried out close to St. Anne's Church uncovered the remains of two large rectangular pools. These are the Pools of Bethesda, as described in John 5:2. Here Jesus performed one of his miracles, healing a crippled man. Colonnades divided the pools into sections. It is believed that sheep were washed in one of these pools before they were sacrificed in the Temple.

The Struthion Pool (above)

During the Second Temple period the pool was outside the Antonia Fortress. It was originally used as a water reservoir by the Roman legionnaires serving in the Antonia. Today the pool can be see within the Convent of the Sisters of Sion.

St. Anne's Church (below)

This church is one of the best preserved and finest examples of a church built during the Crusader period. It is located near St. Stephen's Gate and is built over a crypt venerated as the birthplace of the Virgin Mary and the home of her parents.

(Previous page 94)

The Dome of the Chapel of the Lithostrotos

The chapel marks the Second Station of the Via Dolorosa. It is located in the Antonia Fortress where Pontius Pilate judged Jesus in a place called Gabbatha (Pavement). (John 19:13).

(Previous page 95)

The Chapel of the Second Station and part of the arch "Ecce Homo" in the Via Dolorosa.

(Facing page 96)

The interior of the dome of the Convent of the Flagellation, The Second Station. Inside the dome is a mosaic of the Crown of Thorns.

The Chapel of the Ecce Homo – Sisters of Sion

The Antonia Fortress

Built by Herod the Great in 36 B.C. in honour of Mark Antony – his friend, the Antonia Fortress was destroyed by Titus in 70 A.D. The enormous quadrangle had four great towers. The western section of the Antonia was covered by a paved square ("lithostrotos"), which was used by the legionaires for training and for games. Traditionally it is believed that the Place of Judgement ("Praetorium") was on this pavement, where the Roman Procurator, Pontius Pilate condemned Jesus.

Above
Model of the Antonia Fortress.

Below
The arch of "Ecce Homo" in the Convent of the Sisters of Sion.

Facing (p. 99)
Painting of the arch known as Ecce Homo

This is where Pontius Pilate proclaimed, "Behold the Man". Today the left hand smaller arch is included in the Chapel of the Ecce Homo in the Convent of the Sisters of Sion. The larger arch spans part of the Via Dolorosa.

Above
Part of the pavement in the courtyard of the Antonia Fortress, the remains of which are to be found in the Convent of the Sisters of Sion. Traces of the games played by the Roman soldiers are to be found carved in the stones – this part shows "The Game of the King."

The Stone of Basilindia (below)
Markings on the pavement clearly show evidence of the "King's Game" played by the Romen legionaires.

Sisters of Sion

The Convent of the Sisters of Sion on the paved courtyard ("Lithostrotos") of the Antonia Fortress. Here Jesus received the cross.

Above
The Chapel of the Flagellation, where Jesus was scourged at the pillar.

Below
Part of the pavement named in Greek "Lithostrotos" (Gabbatha). The spot where Jesus faced Pontius Pilate, the Roman Procurator. *"And Pilate gave sentence that it should be as they required."* (Luke 23:24)

Via Dolorosa

The stages of Jesus' last walk and the events that took place on the way to the crucifixion are indicated by Fourteen Stations of the Cross. Nine of these points are actually along the Via Dolorosa and five are inside the Church of the Holy Sepulchre.

Above
A relief of Jesus falling under the weight of the cross at the **Third Station**. This site belongs to the Armenian Catholics.

Below
The Fourth Station – The Church of Our Lady of the Spasm. This is the place where Jesus, carrying the cross, was met by His mother – the Virgin Mary.

Above
The Fifth Station – This is where Simon of Cyrene helped Jesus carry the cross.

Below
The Sixth Station – According to tradition the Sixth Station is revered as the place where Jesus was helped by Veronica, when she wiped the dust and dirt from His face. The imprint of Jesus' face was left on the cloth that Veronica used.

Top right
The Seventh Station – where Jesus fell a second time under the weight of the cross.

Below
The Eighth Station – the Church of St. Charalambos. This is where Jesus turned to the women of Jerusalem saying: *"Weep not for Me, but for yourselves and your children."* (Luke 23:28)

Top left
The Ninth Station – where Jesus fell for the third time. The site is marked by a column built into the door of the Coptic Church.

*Russian excavations. Part of the Atrium of
Constantine's Church of the Holy Sepulchre*

The Church of The Holy Sepulchre

The Church of the Holy Sepulchre was first built by order of the Emperor Constantine the Great, immediately following the Council of Nicaea (325 A.D.). The tomb of Jesus was discovered by the Empress Helena, mother of Constantine. The place was revealed to her in a dream while she was on a visit to Jerusalem. Three different buildings were erected on the spot: A round church called the Anastasis above the empty grave of Jesus; a magnificent basilica called the Martyrium; and in the square between the two churches, a shrine marking the position of the crucifixion, named Calvarium (Golgotha). These buildings were destroyed by the Persians in 614 A.D. They were rebuilt and once more destroyed by Caliph Hakim in 1009 A.D. They were partially restored once more, then in 1149 A.D. the Crusaders, after the conquest of Jerusalem, erected the present church, which has the tomb of Jesus and the place of crucifixion under one roof.

facing page

The exterior of the Church of the Holy Sepulchre

overleaf Page 108

The Tenth Station – Golgotha – where Jesus was stripped of His clothes; and **The Eleventh Station** – where he was nailed to the cross.

The Twelfth Station — Calvary — where Jesus died on the Cross — *overleaf (p. 110)*

The Thirteenth Station *(facing p. 108)* – where Jesus was taken down from the cross. This can be prayed at the Virgin Mary of Sorrows *(below)* or at the Stone of Anointing *(Unction) overleaf p. 111,* where His body was laid out and prepared for burial.

(overleaf p. 112)
The exterior of the Inner Tomb – called the Chapel of the Angel.

(overleaf p. 113)
The Chapel of the Angel. The outer chamber of the Tomb of Christ where the angel first proclaimed the good news of Easter Synday.

(overleaf p. 114)
The Tomb of Christ. The sacred rock is covered by marble. Here the body of Jesus lay from Good Friday until Easter Sunday.

Many different sects practise their religious ceremonies in Jerusalem

View of Jerusalem – The Dome of the Rock *(facing page)*

Above
The hill on which the Garden Tomb is situated. The hill resembles a human skull; for this reason Charles Gordon believed that this was Golgotha.

Below
The Garden Tomb

"Now in this place where He was crucified there was a garden; and in the garden a new sepulchre, wherein was never man yet laid." (John 19:41) Many Protestants believe that the site outside the walls of Jerusalem, north of the Damascus Gate, is the place of the Crucifixion and the Resurrection of Jesus. This site was discovered by the British General Charles Gordon in 1883.

Emmaus "Despised people"

The exact location of this site is not known. It is believed to be the little settlement about 16 kilometres west of Jerusalem.

Above
Part of the Roman road connecting Emmaus with Jerusalem.

Below
The Church of Emmaus (El Qubeibeh)

"And behold, two of them went that day to a village called Emmaus, which was from Jerusalem about three-score furlongs." (Luke 24:13) At Emmaus, Jesus met Cleophas and Simon after His Resurrection and ate with them. The Franciscans built a church on the spot where Cleophas' house was believed to have stood. Others believe that the site of Emmaus is where the Trappist Monastery at Latrun now stands.

A painting in the Church at Emmaus depicting Jesus breaking bread while eating with Simon and Cleophas.

The Dome of the Rock

This mosque was built by Abd El Malik ibn Mirwan, the Omayad Khalif, in 691 A.D. The mosque was built on the site of the First and Second Temples.

One of the entrances to the magnificent mosque encased in marble slabs and Persian tiles, some of which are inscribed with passages from the Koran. *(facing page)*

Right
One of the beautiful stained glass windows in the mosque.

Below
"Solomon's Stables."

Facing page
Es-Sakhra – The Rock on Mount Moriah

The rock on the top of Mount Moriah is in the centre of the Dome of the Rock which is one of the most beautiful and important mosques in the Moslem world. It is built, according to Jewish tradition, on the rock on which Abraham was about to sacrifice his son, Isaac. Here stood the Ark of the Covenant in the First Temple. The rock is holy to Moslems as well; according to their tradition, Mohammed ascended to heaven on his winged steed from here.

The Beautifully Decorated Cupola in the Dome of the Rock

The wood lined cupola is richly decorated with stucco, painted in red and gold. A silver candelabra once hung from the centre; all that remains now is the great chain. Inscriptions from the Koran around the cupola include *"God, there is no God but He, the Living, the Everlasting....."*

The Interior of the Mosque of El-Aksa

This mosque is situated on the southern part of the Temple
Mount, on Mount Moriah. It was built between 709 – 715 A.D.
by Caliph Waleed, son of Abd El Malik. The mosque stands over
an underground building called the Ancient Arcade. The roof
rests on beautifully decorated pillars and arches and the floor is
covered with priceless rugs. The Crusaders used the mosque as a
residence for the knights in charge of the Temple Area. These
knights became known as the Templars. After the defeat of the
Crusaders Saladin restored it as a mosque.

The Gates in the Ancient City Wall.

"Our feet shall stand within thy gates, O Jerusalem."
(Psalms 122:2)

The Golden Gate

This gate is situated on the site of the original Eastern Gate of the Temple Compound. It is a seventh century Byzantine structure. According to Christian tradition Jesus passed through this gate when entering Jerusalem with His Disciples on Palm Sunday. Since the ninth century the gate has been walled up.

Damascus Gate *(right)*

The Damascus Gate in the northern wall was built by Suleiman the Magnificent over the remains of the previous gates. The original site was that of a Herodian structure, followed in 135 A.D. by an entrance into Hadrian's Aelia Capitolina. The Damascus Gate is one of the most impressive and decorative gates in the walls of the Old City.

Top left, **Herod's Gate** in the northern wall.

Top right, **The Dung Gate** in the southern wall.

Bottom left, **The New Gate** in the northen wall.

Bottom right, **St. Stephen's Gate** (also called Lion's Gate)
in the eastern wall.

The Zion Gate in the southern wall, showing damage from fighting between Jordanians and Israelis.

The Citadel (below)

The Citadel adjoins Jaffa Gate. It is one of the most well-known landmarks of Jerusalem. It was once the fortress that guarded Herod's Palace. Today the Museum of the City of Jerusalem is located inside the Citadel and exhibitions are held frequently. Another attraction is a "Sound and Light" show telling the story of the Citadel through all its periods.

"The Tower of David" in Herod's Citadel

The Citadel was built by Herod. Within it were three towers which he called after the people he loved – Mariamne, his wife; Phasael, his brother; and Hippicus, his friend. Of these three towers only the bottom half of one tower remained after the destruction of the city by the Romans. In the last few years excavations carried out have unearthed remains as far back as the Hasmonean period. The Minaret Tower from a later period is erroneously known as the "Tower of David." It was used as a Moslem prayer house and is called by the Arabs "David's Prayer Cell," as Moslem tradition believes that David prayed here.

(Facing p. 131)
Prayers at the Western Wall on weekdays and festivals.

The Shrine of the Book

The Shrine of the Book at the Israel Museum contains the priceless biblical scrolls and scroll fragments found at Qumran. The building was especially designed and erected to symbolize the circumstances of this discovery.

(right)
The interior of the Shrine of the Book.

Below
The Dome of the Shrine of the Book, built like the cover of the jars within which were found the scrolls. The black basalt wall symbolizes the Sons of Darkness – whilst the Shrine itself is a sparkling white for The Sons of Light (the Essenes). In the background, Israel's Parliament – the Knesset – can be clearly seen.

The Model of Ancient Jerusalem in the Grounds of the Holyland Hotel.

Professor Avi Yonah of the Hebrew University put many years of research and work into producing this model of the City of Jerusalem at the time of the Second Temple. The scale model is constructed mainly from the original materials used in the buildings it represents - ie. marble, stone, copper and wood. The splendid Second Temple dominates the scene of Jerusalem's magnificence and beauty in 66 A.D.

The Bedouin *(Overleaf p. 136)*

Bedouin hospitality is well known – in winter guests are welcomed to a tent of woven goats' hair, in summer they are protected from the hot rays of the sun by a thatched shelter. The nomadic lifestyle of these people arouses wonder and curiosity in all who belong to the Western World. The laws governing Bedouin society are almost identical to the laws of Moses. Clothing, food and customs have changed little since Biblical times. Raising livestock, especially camels, sheep and goats, is the traditional occupation of these nomadic people. Farming is not a main source of income. The lack of good soil and the lack of rainwater are not conducive to the growing of crops.

The Bedouin are a healthy, happy people, able to relax and enjoy life despite the harsh conditions under which they live.

Hebron

The Cave of Machpelah *(above)*

The mosque at Hebron is built upon the Cave of the Machpelah, which, according to tradition, contains the tombs of Abraham and Sarah, Isaac and Rebecca and Jacob and Leah. Parts of the mosque are remains of a Herodian building.

Below
Symbolic cenotaphs set above the cave – mausoleum of the Patriarchs and Matriarchs.

(Facing page 138)

Jacob's Well

The well is situated in the crypt of the church which was built by Helena, mother of the Emperor Constantine. The first church was destroyed and a second one, rebuilt by the Crusaders, was also destroyed. Jesus, on His way to the Galilee, arrived at Samaria weary from His journey. He sat down by the well that Jacob had given to his son Joseph when a Samaritan woman came to draw water. Jesus said to her: *"Give me to drink."* (John 4:3-26)

Above
The Mosque of Al Jazzar Pasha in Acre.

Acre *(below)*

Acre, also known as Ptolemais, was an important city and harbour during the period of the Crusaders. *"And when we had finished our course from Tyre we came to Ptolemais, and saluted the brethren, and abode with them one day."* (Acts 21:7)

Caesarea

The Ancient Harbour (above)

The city was built by Herod on the shores of the Mediterranean and named after Caesar Augustus. Caesarea was one of the most splendid cities of the ancient world – filled with all the luxuries that made up Graeco-Roman culture – an amphitheatre, a theatre, a hippodrome and hot baths to name but a few. Remains of the vast harbour can still be seen.

Tiberias – General View (below)

Tiberias – the capital of the lower Galilee is situated 209 metres below sea-level on the south-west shore of the Kinneret. It was founded about 20 A.D. by Herod Antipas the son of Herod the great. Although Tiberias was situated within the radius of Jesus' Ministery, Christianity did not make much headway here until the Byzantine rule of the sixth century. Many of the Gospel stories took place around this area of Galilee.

Haifa

The city is built above the harbour on the slopes of Mount
Carmel. The landscape is dominated by the gold-plated dome
of the Bahai Temple set in the formal Persian gardens. This is
the centre of the Bahai faith which stresses the Unity of God
and the Brotherhood of Mankind.

Jaffa – looking towards Tel Aviv *(facing p. 142)*

Jaffa is the biblical town of Joppa. According to legend Jaffa was founded by Japhet, the son of Noah. The story of Jonah and the whale is associated with Jaffa, from where Jonah set off for his journey to Tarshish. (Jonah 1-17) Here Peter restored Tabitha and *"tarried for many days with one Simon the Tanner."* (Acts 9:43)

From ancient Jaffa the coastline of modern Tel Aviv is clearly visible. The palms are replaced by high-rise concrete buildings. There is a hustle and bustle which is completely different to the serenity of Jaffa. Tel Aviv is the commercial and cultural centre of Israel.

Eilat

Eilat is the town at the head of the Gulf of Eilat opening into the Red Sea. It was first mentioned in Numbers 33:35. Life in Eilat was always quiet, until communications improved, and it became an integral part of the rest of the country. In mid-1967 Eilat started to flourish. Tourists flocked to the shanty town to admire The incredible all-the-year-round summer temperatures, the attractions of sun, sea, water-sports, good hotels and night-life have all contributed towards the economic development of Eilat. Today it is a popular holiday resort and a base for touring to enjoy the sights and wonders of the desert.

(Above) Eilat, underwater scenery in the Red Sea.

(Below) Untamed beauty of the surrounding desert.